Also published by Patrick Hunt

Caravaggio 2004
House of the Muse 2005
Rembrandt 2006
Alpine Archaeology 2007
Ten Discoveries That Rewrote History 2007
Myths for All Time 2007
Renaissance Visions: Myth and Art   2008
Poetry in the Song of Songs 2008

Cloud Shadows of Olympus

Collected Poems from 2006-2009

Patrick Hunt

Pirene Press

First published in the United States of America in 2009
by Pirene Press, an imprimatur of the Corinthian Publishing Group,
San Francisco, California

Library of Congress Cataloging in Publication data

Hunt, Patrick N.,
    Cloud Shadows of Olympus/Patrick Hunt
    Collected poems 2006-2009

ISBN – 978-0-578-04675-4

Typeset in Garamond

Printed and bound in the United States

Front cover art is from an original painting commissioned for this book
from Beatrice Hunt

www.pirenepress.com
www.corinthianpress.com

Preface & Acknowledgments

In Greek Mythology, the Pirene Spring has many stories told about its imaginary history. At Corinth in Greece, the remains of the Pirene Fountain can still be seen within its ancient marble precinct. One story says the famous winged horse Pegasus created the high fountain when his foot struck the mountain of Corinth, similar to Mount Helikon; another that Pegasus was caught by Bellerophon at this Pirene spring at the foot of the mountain of Corinth; yet another story relates how the Muses drank from its water. Many Classical writers wrote about or praised the Pirene (or Peirene) for its role in inspiration for the Western imagination, among them, Ovid, Strabo, Pliny, Plautus, Statius and Pausanias, among ancient sources, and Milton among later writers. Thus it is satisfying that this poetry, mostly about antiquity, is now published by Pirene Press. My sources are not only from cherished experience and reading as well as exploring ancient sites known from archaeology and related literature, much of it lyrical or mythological, but also from art both ancient and modern, where artists have made their own visual commentary on subjects or myth. These poems are often ekphrastic in the sense that they allude to other tellings and retellings, where art inspires art.

The poems collected in this small volume were written in the last few years, following publication of House of the Muse (2005), and previous collections, Arepo the Sower (1980) and Wings Over Hellas (1990), for the most part the present poems are unpublished until now. The following poems have been recently published outside this volume and are reprinted here by courtesy: "Kithairon" in *The Penguin Book of Classical Myths*, 2008; "Delphi" by the American School of Classical Studies, Athens, 2009; "Garden of Cyrus" by the World Academy of Art, Literature and Media, London, 2009;

"Pomona's Season" by the Classical Association of the U.K. (Britain), 2009. Other poems are forthcoming as individual publications in *Amphora* (American Philology Association), *Aethlon,* and *Modern Age: A Quarterly Review.*

This small book of poetry is dedicated with gratitude and humility to many who have pointed the way, particularly the following individuals:

To colleagues, friends and mentors like Herant and Stina Katchadourian, Helen Bing, Cordell Hull, Riva Tooley, John Felstiner, Jenny March, Scotty McLennan, Mike Keller, Bill Durham, Irving Finkel, Richard Martin, Rush Rehm and John Fischer. I could not have asked for deeper affirmations of life, erudite guidance and profound reminders of unwavering purpose.

To my Stanford students, especially the following in 2009, who inspired me and offered their own insights as we studied Classics together, in alphabetical order: Aparna A., Ashley C., Jeremy C., David G., LiHe H., Tom H., Lina H., Moya M., Zach O'K., Paul P., Lilian R., Ethan S., Annie S., John S., and Flora W.

To my publisher at Pirene Press, a division of the Corinthian Publishing Group, Richard Reed (D.Phil., Oxford) for his tireless vision and courage to champion literary creation.

Above all to my wife Pamela and our three daughters Hilary, Allegra and Beatrice, (Three Graces) through all our family's often quixotic peregrinations gifted with their embrace of adventure. Without their patient love and trust, any words here are meaningless.

Patrick Hunt
2009

Table of Contents

Table of Contents (cont.)

Tragoedia

for Rush Rehm

Priests of Dionysus drag a wild-eyed goat
kicking all the way to the theater,
stopping at a marble altar draped in ivy.
Tying the goat with hemp ropes against its will,
its struggling hooves tattoo only air
with a lone dithyrambic drum sounding
as the falling knife seeks its own rhythm
too quick for human eye to follow.
Nearly all can see an arc of blood
almost as purple as the god's,
all hear the goat's dark scream.
A choking death rattle chills the air
but all the waiting god hears is music,
goat song, tragoedia. While audiences
straining shocked ears, cannot see
or hear the god's stately yet lurching steps
his slow dance from temple to theater,
dread silences the crowd as the play,
another drama, can only now begin.

Fishmarket Krater

Above Cefalu harbor a Greek story
painted on Mandralisca's krater
offers several outcomes being netted.
In the fishmarket two men gesture,
each trying to cut a better deal.
One whole tuna drips on the floor,
unable to swim away again.
But another plump tuna is divided
by a skinny old fish merchant,
sharp as his knife. The blade is raised
high for a third slice above this tuna
whose head is already separated
from its body, mouth agape
as if in gilled conversation
with its finny schoolmate,
not in deep water but shallow air,
perhaps discussing breathless fate.
The buyer dickers over price,
his hand and pained expression
suggest he feels he's being gouged
more than the fish. His preference
has changed, too many drachma
for not enough fish, see the nick
where the merchant had begun his cut.
We cannot know the outcome
although two Greek proverbs wag:
the merchant's knife raised high
may cut the careless buyer,
thus injury follows insult. The other
proverb, no less ambidextrous,
warns this buyer to keep
on the right side of the blade.

Aeschylos in Gela

for Marsh McCall

Aeschylos walked metrically in Gela
acting out a new play as he strode
through tall cypresses, plotting
paradox, episodes, chorus laments
about Icarus flying close to the sun
and his featherless fall from on high.

Eyeing the resting dramatist who had
paused with his papyrus by his side,
flying above the poet was a young eagle
who knew all about wings needing wind
more than wax, less about drama and destiny.
From a hundred foot height he dropped

a turtle on Aeschylos' head and broke
the poet's round sky-filled cranium,
the dramatist's last inspiration from on high
not mythic but the sudden weight of reality.
How could the master of tragedy know
he would eventually become one?

Princess of Vix

for Bruno Racine

Looking for new markets overseas
Greeks traded lordly wine to Gauls,
amphorae dragged from long ships
to far domains where Celtic bards
praised such potent juice. Gaulish kings

drank with elation but were assured
mortals could only handle so much
of this divine gift, with no such limits
in the next life. Plus, it would make
their sunless underworld less dark.

This is why one wise princess of Vix
took to her Celtic grave a giant krater,
bronze masterpiece made in distant Rhodes.
But it wasn't treasured for its craft:
it held enough wine for a fete in Elysium,

assuring her a welcome there, sufficient
to twice fill over seven hundred cups
and make every farmer's well echo
under fields of Chatillon-sur-Seine
with drinking songs for centuries.

Virgil's Bees

for Sandro Barchiesi

Virgil's bees hum bucolics in our ears,
swarms sharing common sunny notes
when nothing is more prized than honey.
Vibrating wings fan air in woven osier hives
bearing gold rich pollen no one else
would think to hoard. For millennia
like doctor sages, bees have diagnosed
violet gardens for us or an old oak's hollow,
fragrant boles of salvia and blue borage,
wild mountain thyme high on dizzy cliffs
only they and sun can touch. They dance
from giddy haze to greener shade
where streams sing through clovered swards
and toads serenade their mates from lotuses.
Architect bees mix pollen and tasty wax,
building towered houses for themselves,
in their mathematic way calculate distance
and compass between nectar and their queen
in semaphore for where good sources lie
relative to their hive. For all their piloting
through air, bees never crash into each other
and if like legionnaires they carry sword,
are apt to sacrifice for queen and colony,
dulce et decorum est pro colonia mori but always
sweeter to live. No one caresses roses
like a bee, or if blossoms be her nipples,
sucks so passionate at earth's breast,
bending a flower with the weight of desire.

Life of Sappho

for Carolyn Lougee

Small and dark like an olive
hidden among silver leaves
ripened by wind and sun,

as a girl dressed in white linen
in a lordly house where laughter
poured alongside noble wine,

Sappho would not stand out
until her eyes flashed
and then her glance could fell

anyone. If Sappho held a word
like honey softly in her mouth,
rolling it with her tongue,

letting it rest behind white teeth
for a moment, her imagination
could create beauty gods might envy

or if jilted in love, spurned
for someone else male or younger
her fierce words were bitter

as salt water pouring foam
over limestone on Lesbos shore
where sandpipers always mourn.

Carving a plectrum for her kithara
to seize strings in strident hexachords,
she invented new lyric stanzas

now named for her. She laughed
at gold unless it was in dawn skies,
untouchably light. Eulogized by larks

more than nightingales who praise evening,
Sappho hated to be alone in bed or cold
when two could share body warmth.

Wedded to lavender or apricot
more than men, she always smiled
to smell apples dear as roses,

and if girls were lovely to her sight,
it was intense desire for beauty,
Aphrodite herself she wanted most.

Whinnying horses tossed their heads
and fountains in dappled sunlight
sang to her, lyrics she softly hummed

when by herself, and gods listened.
Surrounded by girls who adored her
power over them, fond of even her tantrums,

Sappho counted stars like notes of music,
lovers sculpted by moonlight, flowers
hardly noticed by anyone else,

blooms short-lived as youth.
Her eyes were her singular feature,
changing color in a moment,

sometimes gray seas under clouds
or fresh green as spring myrtle
or hot as smoldering amber

depending on her mood. Some swore
her voice could imitate winds
or high bird cries from cliffs

as if Circe wove her magic, all
because Sappho knew well
how to hoard wealth in a poem,

her narratives full of splendid images:
sight, sound, smell, touch, taste found
in her hymns like fruit in rich orchards

or markets where spices beckon,
cinnamon breathes, perfumes caress
nostrils, balsam glows, lilies sway.

When Sappho played at weddings
longing as much or more after brides
as for their grooms, she often groaned

at losing bosom friends to bedrooms
she would never see again, shedding tears
of anguish for maidenheads taken,

kisses she could never share, banished
from warm breasts where she could not
rest her head, from friends whose dances ended.

Married to a cipher from Andros
only to bear her beloved daughter Kleis,
Sappho kept him away whenever possible,

saying those seas were too rough for him
to cross, or that her priestess duties
kept her far busier than she wished.

Ironic about her own aging in mirrors,
Sappho mocked death, fiercely ribbing it
as a dubious thing immortals shunned.

Whether she leapt off a cliff after
a tawny fisherboy or just withered away,
the Muses welcomed their eternal sister.

Pomona's Season

for Jenny March

Pomona finishes her season,
swelling fruit to perfection,
pears resembling breasts
dripping with sweet milk,
soft figs passable for testes
full of seed, every harvest
desirable. It is hard for her
to leave duty at its climax,
but her work is done
calling golden bees to pollinate
shy flowers, inviting sun
and wind to nourish labor
from early spring to summer's end.
Only one ill could undo
her blessings: if her ripe fruits
are uneaten, hanging lonely
on trees beyond their time
or fallen to hard ground.
If this happens, such a place
does not know Pomona's love
or the voice of her Vertumnus
who always comes disguised
until autumn's light bends.
In their orchard she makes sure
every bright apple is plucked,
each bite savored until its last.
Then Pomona smiles, satisfied,
climbing in her woody bed to sleep
until her dreams turn green again.

Descartes Unwaxed

for Jeremy Sabol

Held wax warms to touch, changing form
but not nature, mollifying wings of thought
as aspiring Icarus found, loose feathers
of his will unable to maintain direction

in all but one of three dimensions, heavenly
body suddenly earthbound. Put a candle
to wax and it melts, although it might take
a little longer in Stockholm than in Rome

where canons fume over a doubter's discourses.
Cartesian coordinates stretch his mind's map
along new geometric pathways, since logic
is no longer linear, not perverse or bent but curved

like a breast, a much more desirable conclusion.
If Descartes decides that God exists beyond
his senses, who are we to find his syllogism
empty when we cannot see any better than he

what light hides behind darkness. Even while
sun appears behind clouds, not often enough
for him in Baltic climes, his last pneumonic cough
was eloquent, because then he saw with eyes closed.

What Winds Whisper Through Trees

for W. S. Merwin

What winds whisper through trees
rustling leaves at sylvan Dodona
have tuned few subtle ears to gods
who appreciate ambiguity. Their oracles

are intelligible to those who know
that when winds moan through groves
they may not lament human affairs
and trifles of kings and armies

but maybe death of old forests
when axes bite deep into sacred wood
and torn mossy earth cries out underneath
until all seeds and creatures migrate away

and songbirds fly west forever
far from human voices and where
only waves converse with wet rocks
rounded and hidden under cliffs.

Priests of Zeus harvest acorns
under oaks after heavy storms,
counting them to find answers
when winds offer only ambiguity,

too soft to understand what oracles
imply without clear trends in any direction,
numerical accounting in exchange
for literality is emptily problematic.

Leaves turn in soft breezes
to sun that will soon angle away
in oblique autumn light, knowing
their own lives are but one season

and they do not despair but glory
in changing color, bushes aflame
without burning. Their gods are sun,
moon and stars, water at their roots

and this is enough to whisper
about. Oracles may not be indifferent
to humans but have always mocked
folly of self-importance, vanity

of hierarchies, pretense of altruism
and what passes as new wisdom. Whether
they ever speak without ambiguity,
they can easily read the future

in bird flights, leaf whisperings,
water babbling over river rock,
high signs in darkest heavens,
because they have already read the past.

Memoria

for Principessa Raffadali

Not so long ago, Palermo
was the richest city in the world.
Phoenician sails were sunset gold
across turquoise seas, Greeks brought
dazzling marble, white as snow,
Romans green or purple porphyry,
Moorish mathematicians mapped
the night's high-domed starry sky
and Monreale Valley air was filled
with fragrances of flowering lemons
from the royal groves Boccaccio knew.
But most precious of all Palermo's pearls
is time, memories the Muses cannot lose
nor countless Mediterranean waves erase.

Hylas and the Nymphs

While other Argonaughts rested,
no matter that heroes sometimes do,
young Hylas walks out alone seeking water
to refresh them all. Mysia had dark woods,

deep springs bubbling fresh, willows
drinking at their roots whose silvery leaves
speared light where any penetrated.
Pegae is a quiet spring covered

with water lilies white and blue
floating on its surface, yellow iris
fingering air, lazy insects droning by
in dappled light above dark water.

Hylas wanders here, hears a splash
amid bent reeds to peer at ripples
lifting lily pads where he wonders
if water laughed a moment before.

He is brave on land, hard muscled
from wrestling, knows battle even in his teens,
but Hylas cannot swim. He holds his
hydria vessel down, bending far over.

Suddenly an underwater hand
catches his arm, pulling up until a nymph
appears, paler than any lily by her ear,
wet hair streaming, but more beautiful

than painted, bejeweled women
he had glimpsed in golden palaces.
This dripping water nymph needs
no other ornament than her smile.

With little water rills other nymphs
now surface beside Hylas, surrounding
his tongue of grassy bank, only solid
bit of earth around their spring.

But their dark eyes are deeper
than their water, dilated from sunless
dwellings underneath, whispered voices
laughing at his handsome youthfulness.

Hylas does not know that water nymphs
are always loneliest of all immortals, no one
else can breathe underwater except fish,
and they need young Hylas urgently

to fertilize their cool eggs, waiting
centuries inside their wet nests for
a warm youthful mortal like this
who will bring them his sunlit seed.

He cannot fathom what they say
but hears pleading as they stroke
his arms, tethering him there beside
water, their slender arms root strong.

Washing over him was their desire,
amoral hunger, its purity no issue,
shaking their high breasts at him
and even caressing themselves

and him simultaneously. Immortal,
never looking older than his younger
sister, hypnotic in desire these daughters
of Dryope begin kissing Hylas on his arms,

gently but firmly pulling him downward,
now their full lips warm on his chest.
He gasps when one nymph bites his finger,
her nipples hard against his stomach.

Poor Hylas groans, head swimming
as swarming nymphs fondle him
even between his legs that they now have
touching water, weakening his last anchor.

Hylas hears far away his name called,
Herakles come searching, "Hylas, Hylas",
this hero loves him like a son,
and only when its sound grows louder,

like a flower, one bold nymph opens
her legs around him, holding him inside,
then every nymph pulls Hylas down
together into their darkness of deep water.

Only bubbles rise to surface from below
responding to a hero's voice, finally subsiding
when Herakles calls out near, water silent
because drowned young Hylas is never found.

Monreale

Ten thousand times ten thousand tessera of gold
are heaven's bright witnesses to creation,
Adam's dream of helpmate, seeds to plant
and children born before mortality struck.

Arks of animals and camel caravans float
in glory under high roof, miracles everywhere
of saints who gathered on Monreale's mount
for their own transfiguration, a firmament

placed tile on patient tile by Byzantine mosaicists
who sailed from monasteries on the Bosporus
to work with Arab architects for Norman lords,
Christ Pantocrator hearing the mix of tongues

before him with the faintest smile, less stern
because the apse he rests in, its interior mosaics
inlaid in geometric traceries of strong stone,
soars over the blue conch of Palermo far below.

Arethusa

for Baron Pietro Beneventano del Bosco

Whoever was chasing her lithe nymph grace,
dancing feet leaping woody hills, he too was
goathoofed sure and straight across Alpheus Gorge.
But his mind was beastly bent and gnarled,
thickened old bark compared to her sapling skin.
Knotted hands stretched out to grasp her softness,
desiring her mossy places, her pursuer
did not expect her divine last second rescue
a surge of river covering her long dive
into a foaming waterfall met by mist
before it plunged to darkness underground.
Arethusa disappeared forever, leaving Greece
but her sweet spring bubbled up oversea
at Ortygia, her river lover hard behind her.
Now she murmurs amidst nodding reeds
on her island off Siracusa, papyrus rustling
when good winds tousle her hair, dolphins
nuzzling Arethusa's watery face. Migrating birds
nest in her coolness when all the sun's fire
is mirrored against clear blue water below,
inspiring her favorite son Archimedes
to defend her from the lusts of conquest.

Fortuna Siciliana

Past the cathedral, under Noto's Baroque limestone eaves of griffin and winged horse balconies groaning heavily with history, where all spice and nut sellers gather in shade, a strange smiling gypsy boy hawking fortunes found me beside the palm tree. Or was he a gnome, maybe even a monkey? I may never know, since his features kept changing. He held out one brown hand for a silver coin, the other held an ornately carved coral and pearl box housing a colored parakeet, I think, or was it a baby phoenix, its ruby and sapphire feathers spreading light like a prism? The bird opened a gilded drawer with its gold beak and picked out a folded paper Sicilian fortune for me. How could I refuse? Unfolded, it puzzled my eyes. When I looked up for help, the gnomish boy was gone. My fortune pictured a starry-robed, diamond-spectacled wizard in conical red hat and long beard offering a giant key, but swirling around him was an illusion of impossible depth that made me dizzy. Here were galaxies of incoherent symbols, pentagrams, magic squares, hieroglyphs and numbered gibberish. I counted words, turning the fortune upside down, reading it backwards and sideways. Under the wizard, a green lizard winked at me from its amethyst eye. Through a confusion of scripts, I saw glimmers of Old Romany, High Celtic, Gothic, Cyrilic, Kufic Arabic, Antiochan Greek, Armenian, Pontic Latin, Nestorian, Baghdad Hebrew and Sanskrit. Finally, when I rubbed my eyes, the emerald green lizard climbed up from the paper, running over my arm to my shuddering shoulder where he whispered these words to me in a thin voice like dry ancient parchment: "All the planets of true fortune reveal you are a sympathetic figure, torn by doubts. What you seek can only be yours by the strongest desire and force of will. Do not let malignant envy feed on your soul or nemesis shadow your smile until it fades away like youth. Be confident your deepest treasure, hope, will always be invisible to others but a lighthouse to you in your deepest tribulations. Be courageous and no shipwreck will suck you under its dark wave! Conquer yourself!" The lizard's whisper faded away. He ran back down my arm, leaping into the paper, becoming smaller again as he shut his lavender eye. A capricious breeze tore the colored paper fortune from my hand, refolding it like wings. The folded paper fortune transformed into a butterfly, flying away smaller and smaller into the future.

Agrigento

Once eagles circled piny ridges over Agrigento,
their geometry of air a compass for sun
and wind following their wings. Other circles
ripple outward from Greek columns

fluted by templed light and shadow,
brightly vertical against a blue horizon
seen between them. The valley below
remembers Pindar's most beautiful city,

thick old olive trees hollowed by time
hold ancient pottery fragments in their roots,
painted amphorae where artists entwined vines
around storied myth, where living capers

and wild figs now spread over fertile soil,
making their own leafy mosaics as if
extending buried dreams of walls underneath
and floors that wait for drumming feet again.

Clouds

for W. S. Merwin

Clouds add more than color to sky, lending depth
to air's imagination, giving sun a watercolor palette
to invent anew, breaking blue monotonies,
creating sculpture for a moment or two. Brooms
of cirrus sweep up high, thunderheads tower to full height,
mackerel scales fan and swim, nimbus glowers
in mutiny where it can flood a sky, shy stratus hides
within itself to make invisible anything within it.
Tropical clouds duplicate their own dark forests above
lush vegetation. Mountain clouds hem in rocky peaks
far harder than themselves. Prairie clouds fly in flocks,
wings outstretched to far horizons, as fulsome
as the plain below is flat. Whether storing water
or bringing shade, clouds dapple landscapes like sheep
with shade grazing below them. When we lay down
to watch clouds pass overhead, we are humbled
by comparison to even smallest clouds, and far richer
than those too distracted to look up, misers of their eyes
who will be poor even in sunlight. Persons we call
blind say they can even feel a cloud shadow passing,
proving they're not blind at all, like bees sensing other
wavelengths vibrating through a thousand eye lenses
or heat through quivering antennae we should envy.
Clouds may even be alive, a population we can't count,
often traveling in thick clans, families on the move
predicting weather wordlessly, almost weightless
like guardian angels watching over us as they fly quietly,
citizens of sky as we are citizens of earth.

Selinunte

Not wild celery by the greener sea,
sun ripening in fields Demeter blessed,
but now red poppies wreathe Selinunte,
its towering gates and monumental walls
where Kotone harbor sheltered ships
from every colony, hull jostling hull

in sea breezes. Great temples
overshadowed long white streets
where sailors gawked at maidens
and olive oil flowed like rivers
as priests muttered prayers to gods
through rising clouds of incense.

Seabirds rather than Greek navies
sail along its sandy coast now
where Selinunte's once teeming throngs
and unctuous corner merchants are replaced
by an oblivious legion of ants on the march
or a few lizards sunning on stone ruins.

Bacchus Transformed

for Jake Mackey

Marc Antony spent huge sums on wine,
enough to stagger anyone. In the Senate
when he spoke, words poured out equal
to what he poured in, usually just as senseless.
Hiring a marble sculptor to render himself
as Bacchus, he often dressed this way for parties,
Antony's features played across the god's mask:
infamous weak chin drooling with beard,
eyes squinting to discern one person from
a triumvir of competing images, mocking smile
more a rictus. Holding up a cluster of grapes
in one hand and his ever ready cup in another,
his statue was placed in Antony's villa on Naxos,
apropros locus as Dionysus' sacred isle.
While Rome dissipated and Theodosius
brushed away old religion as empty paganism,
Christianity could have no competition,
so Antony's statue as Bacchus toppled. After
his own likeness was forgotten except on coins,
Antony slept. But how surprised might later
Christians be, communing with their new god
through Eucharistic cups, to know their
venerated Christ statue in a medieval church
was resurrected from Antony as Bacchus?
Some still hear Antony laughing at this trinity.

Segesta

Here birds sing to improbable gods
no unison chant but a chatter of wind,
dancing sounds, mountain amplified.

What gods these birds understand
must also have beautiful wings,
blue as heaven and gold as dawn.

Shadows lean into morning
led by sun into unfinished columns
where roof is sky, floor is rock

and faroff vines feed these deities
whose voices still echo in storms
rolling from the sea. Once or twice

in a human lifetime, a fleeting moment
for immortals, gods' usually hidden faces
may be seen high in clouds over Segesta.

Beards

for Irving Finkel

"A Babylonish dialect which learned
pedants much affect." (Hudibras 1.93)

Beards flow through Jerusalem, long Hasidic ones
powdered with limestone temple dust, beards where
Targum scrolls are stored, rabbinic beards echoing
Solomonic proverbs, fanned by wind from angels' wings
on Horeb, or Elijah's beard flaming from sky chariots
desert demons cannot touch. Beards flow through
Babylonian nights, beards forked like horned stars
of gazelle constellations, silent hooves veering high
over Euphrates plains, distant blazing patterns
astrologers mutter and squint at, looking for meaning
illegible on clay. Mysterious beards of Chaldees
bend over livers, haruspex beards tangled with omens,
blood bubbling goat voices leaking from bearded torn
sacrificial throats. Blake saw dazed Nebuchadnezzar's
wild and shaggy beard drag as he crawled on all fours
like an animal, so long it rested on grasses eaten in cracks
of forgotten courtyards. Beards flow through Susa,
pomaded with myrrh, beards dangled like ivy hanging
over walls of Median fortresses. Beards flow like rivers
through Nineveh, braided with knucklebones of slaves,
kingly beards making our teeth chatter in fear
coherent as cuneiform curses, or coiled and oiled beards
like Esarhaddon's, where no manly Assyrian dares

grow one longer than his king or he'll lose both beard
and head above it. Even false beards are attached
in Egypt under shaved heads, fixed but not flowing,
strapped on like leather saddles royal heads ride
with authority, beards curved like cobra tongues or rays of sun
through pools of lotus and mandrakes. Byzantine beards
flow with iconostasis harmony in candlelit gold mosaic domes,
beards orthodox as polyhymnic clouds floating over Mistra.
But no beard as sage as yours, so scholarly it lilts in Elamite
below your mouth as easily as a racing moon reads dunes
or running water reads rock along riverbeds of time.
And when you smile in irony, panthers in your beard stretch
and purr, sheathing their sharp claws under glittering eyes.

Callisto

Following Odysseus through azure seas
around three capes and shores,
where different waves sang
in their siren voices, we feasted
like his sailors both on boat and shore.
We saw amazing undreamt things
after Messina's narrow straits:
tall Etna smoking over us,
towering Cyclopean caves
where flutes echoed, grottoes
like seashell mysteries whispering,
secret gardens of gods, and although
we did not tempt Poseidon that we knew,
we skirted cliffs brewing storms
between whitecapped islands,
mooring in Libyan pirate harbors
where we still slept safe, gently
rocked to sleep until sunlight
beckoned over water each morning
and our eager anchors leapt up
to sail another day round Lilybaeum.

Where Worms Die

for Greg Watkins

Mysterious why a worm dies
on sidewalks after rain,
desiccated by sunshine,
abandoning blind dark safety,
soil keeping it moistly alive
to risk apocalyptic bird beaks
and quickly stiffening light.

Surfacing from a buried life,
opposite us who toil in light
but end in graves and darkness,
you see a worm turning dirt
in a cool garden when it only
rushes to hide, squirming
away from an eyeful world.

Preferring closeness
squeezed between clay
pressing on all sides,
a worm enriches all it eats,
long mouth tasting everything
passing slowly through it,
a thousand shades of truffle.

Normally avoiding light
as accidental nemesis, perhaps
a worm knows its time to die,
nature banishing it from sight until
its end, only seeking a minute of sun
- is heaven blissful or not ? -
once in a worm's lifetime.

Rienzi

for John Deathridge

Rienzi's empire of clouds is lofty
but fleeting, a puff of wind topples
his sky towers. Tribunes need wills
stronger than cuirass bronze
and his vision is dry wood, tinder
for old passions strong as fire.
His is not a Rome whose brick roots
reach deep to Capitoline wells of past dream
but a sputtering lamp without oil tomorrow.
Petrarch may be a friend afar, but nearby
Colonna's name is older, stronger
than Avignon's bridge to nowhere.
Rienzi was content with tides that wash
emperors' bones, they bleach but do not clean,
and old Tiber's river god is muddier
than any from glacial Rhone. On Campidoglio
you hear Rienzi's ghost, pale as smoke,
behind string arpeggios warning
not to promise what cannot be realized,
Wagner's howling demon drums
and trumpets drown all else.

Like Hafez I Always Dream

for Pamela

You and I will be a divan together,
our arms around each other,
wisteria blooms tumbling in waves
in a locked hideaway only we know,
long cascades of purple clusters
intoxicating as heavy grapes hang
in our vineyard where I lie all night
feeding between your lily breasts.

Gardens, orchards or vineyards
are meditations of love and beauty,
lush oases places for our soul.
Good Persian kings chose gardening
over war. At Persepolis in their reliefs
these wise kings hold lotus gently
in hand rather than sword or mace,
pondering ephemera of reigns and empires

and beauty's brevity, where desert flowers
may only last from dawn to sunset
before their petals lose their sheen.
Once a thoughtful Goethe wrote that
Beauty asked God why he made her life
so passing short. His response: only what
is passing has he made beautiful. From high
mountains, springs flow down through valleys

of wind-perfumed orange groves
to fountains of blue tesserae under
burst pomegranates spilling bright seed,
where Damavand's shadows climb palm trees.
Hummingbirds dart, butterflies hover
above mandrakes and aloes share spices.
Like Hafez I always dream of my Beloved
waiting for me even when my bones lie still.

Venice

Piazza San Marco

The sunset bells of Venice sound out
around her city, their joyous noise
rippling in waves through canals

whose secrets last centuries.
Like a virago, Venice has many layers
of rouge covering her beautiful face.

She seduces us in subtle ways, here
an eye of blue sky above or between
tall palaces, there a flash of white teeth

in her smile reflecting sunny water.
Every time we come, helpless
we confess our eternal love for her

at St. Mark's Basilica, whose fragrant incense
curls around domed ceiling mosaics
where gold is the color of heaven on earth.

Pindar's Final Ode

for Irene Romano

Pindar would breathe sweet almond blossoms
one more time through his window,
see silver olive leaves wreathe a moon

for his final ode that night when Hermes came
silently, only a dawn wind whispered
setting star names in his ear. Hermes' staff, pointed

with its mating snakes full of earth magic downward,
touched ground and split it open like a fig
or pomegranate when it falls ripe and full.

Pindar could not lift his old head
when Hermes called but his soul obeyed.
Morning light waiting on his horizon,

one last glance at Argos deep in shadow
and pines southward on distant blue Taygetos
until Pindar followed Hermes' dancing foot

in his soul's own slow cadenza, his outward eye
closing but his inward eye awakening to asphodels
blooming bright at the gate of Elysium.

Lohengrin

Long-necked swans in chorus cry hornlike,
snowy wings thundering across dark water.
What swan boat glides in swirled mist
carrying quiet knight on holy quest? For now
young Gottfried endures his magic state,
hidden heir under his bird guise, hearing
faroff harps sadly plucked by rose thorns
where Philomela sings in starlight.
Since he cannot rule his land in avian form,
no armor shields his soul from wounds
when every feather marks an arrow's entering.
Neither Lohengrin's silence or his sword
keep sorcery at bay or Elsa safe for long.
 Joy's nature ephemeral, sorrow eternal,
asking is forbidden but her answer sadly bidden.
Long before, Leda fathomed tragedy brought
when a swan god's head portended Aphrodite
as Leonardo hinted in that burnt canvas,
flaming wooden horse hatched from eggshells.
Only grim Lohengrin and weeping Elsa exit,
thereby freeing their young duke from swan thrall.
While love's echoes die away in distant brass,
time's mirror ever marries victory with loss.

Corinthian Aphrodite

She overpowers every living thing
at times with desire, even gods melt
in her fire. Apollo himself becomes
irrational in her grip, obsessed with
Sibyl, Cassandra and Hyakinthos
when possessed by her power,
although his love is rarely sated.
No sculptor or painter succeeds
with her likeness, just as she wishes,
every one blinded by her charms,
always acquiescing to her warm pulse.
Dressed only in a few acanthus leaves,
Aphrodite beckons from her temple
atop Corinth, where sailors from every port
throng to worship with her hierodules,
a thousand girls, gifts of grateful Xenophon
home from Persia, barely enough.
She arrived here first on gentle waves
from eastern shores, lux oriente, named
Cypris, Paphian goddess, even earlier
as Astarte, Ishtar and Inanna. Her star
rules night's portals, dawn and dusk,
rosy-fingered and gold. Only sun, moon
are brighter, but if asked whom we could
live without, most of us cannot bear
to exile Aphrodite from rudderless dreams
even when ruled by her exhausting pangs.

Apple

for Scotty McLennan

Cranach's Adam looks confused, scratching
his reddish bearded head, barely making
eye contact with Eve – looking every bit
one naked cognizant. She hands him an apple
because in Latin malum can be ambiguous, meaning
both "apple" and "evil" with only a slight accent
of difference regardless whether this fruit
is golden delicious or tart pippin. Tree of Knowledge
it might be where serpents hang out, subtly
sibilant if even audible, whose tongues are incapable
of consonants like unvoiced apicoalveolars
such as t or soft apicodentals of th and retroflex r
in "truth". This snake can certainly manage u
as a frontal vowel long as his spinal cord
since he has plenty more ribs to spare than Adam.
The snake adroitly twists words like God, dexterous
or sinister. Just like a Snake to tell a little truth
in order to promote a greater lie, although
it's illogical that God could tell a little lie
in order to further greater truth. Whether or not
Adam knows much of anything is dubious,
since he cannot yet fathom historical theology
such as sin or a serpent lifted up in a tree,
which would be ridiculous if Cranach had only
painted what he knew from empirical data.
But apples naturally not only harbor worms,
they also always savor a bit of poison in their seeds,
perhaps for self-preservation. At least as good
a looker as Eve, this apple will be forever toxic,

not just cyanide - carbon triple bonded with nitrogen
- but tasty fructose with essential building blocks
of life in molecular carbon, hydrogen and oxygen,
hence organic. But did God say organic things
always have to die, whether or not the serpent
shared that sweet little morsel of destiny?

Iphigenia

for Chris Ann Matteo

Let the wind's breath die first, others will follow.
Calchas trembles reading stars mirrored on livers,
comets fallen like spears, eclipsed moons
returning with a vengeance. Hordes wait
in doldrums at Aulis with armored restlessness
but when they begin to leave, unraveling the borders
of his dream sails, a vain king loses more
than any false courage their numbers brought him.
Agamemnon has not chosen well so far,
will he sacrifice his pride on this altar,
give up his ships and the praise of men
or further dilute his faint father love?
Whichever is saltier, seawater or blood?
Deaf and blind to Iphigenia's tears,
he will not hear her doe-like cries softening,
he will not even hear either sound or fury
in this new wind slicing like a sword edge.

Gardens

for Robert Harrison

You know where gardens pause
and woods begin, one planned for beauty,
rest or joy; another subtler, undesigned
except by place. Winds and birds
in woods drop random seeds by air,

butterflies wing through either place
searching throats of flowers; blooms await
for fruiting ovaries with bees' help.
Both woods and gardens possess trees,
flowers, shade and water. Surely dragonflies

understand how fountains differ
from springs. Rather than controlling
nature in gardens, imposing order
for its own sake - Eden was no wilderness -
gardening is what greens the soul.

Elijah

Elijah was only a man
but he checked out of here
differently than all of us
who grow still at last
in darkening rooms,
shadows all around, going
with groans or whispers.
Whirlwinds tossed his beard
as chariots of fire swept him up
rushing away with flaming horses
out of sight. His mantle fell off
unneeded, one that smote
old Jordan river and it parted.
We would give almost anything
to depart that way too, perhaps
not melodramatic as opera
but a lot more exciting
than an intravenous drip
and proof our lives meant
something more to heaven
than a prayer in limbo
or an obituary paid to run
a few days after time is useless
to us. Pyromania or not,
Elijah's word never failed,
commanding drought for years,
prophesying Queen Jezebel's end -
dogs licked up her lovely blood -
he mocked manic priests of Ba'al
dancing all day into frenzy,

at times fed only by ravens
in a wilderness. Perhaps
if we lived on road kill
like he did for three years
by lonely Cherith brook,
we too just might merit
being caught up on high
instead of dying of boredom.

Federico, Stupor Mundi

for Conte Alessandro Federico and
Contessa Alwine Federico
Palazzo Conte Federico, Palermo

Mighty eagle, circling higher and higher
against blue Sicilian sky, dared all winds
to stop his outstretched wings: Federico,
world's wonder, crossed swords with Rome
and won. Bringer of peace to Jerusalem,
speaking five languages with a golden tongue,
counted stars by their Arabic names,
wrote canzoni, treatises on falcons, hunting
and courtly love with equal grace. Just,
tolerant, gentle in amor yet fierce in war,
when no other kingdom glittered
under cloudless skies, he planted groves
of scented lemon trees, like King David
sang to his skillful harp and just as easily
tamed leopards. Whatever beast's roar
echoed over Nebrode Mountains,
Federico's wise voice thundered longer.
Our world has never seen his equal.

Etruscan Mirror

for Sandro Barchiesi

Found in a vineyard outside Arezzo,
flaky green bronze disc with no handle
and no reflection for millennia
judging by corrosion. Nothing left

to polish on recto side, verso side etched
with spidery letters. Now in a museum,
thanks to its late translator friend,
a cleaned inscription reads for all:

"This was a parting gift of Porsenna,
a once noble citizen, to his dying wife."
Perhaps she wished to take it to her grave,
hoping that if she could look in it again

down in her golden afterlife banquets,
the way earth weds so quickly to bronze
it would be a kinder image in patina
than she would ever see above. Instead

if you peer closely in her beloved mirror,
you'll see her blooming now in poppies red
between tall cypresses on her tumulus hill
or that poplar in her finest spring green dress.

Semele

Zeus could scrutinize with eagle eyes
from clouds, prescience fogged by desire,
targeting this Theban princess as he plummeted
to land near her bathing in Asopus stream,
a naked young priestess from his rural shrine
who dreamed of pleasing gods by sacrifice
while splashing water over her comely body.
Who can resist when divine persuasion
bends a feeble mortal will to a god's iron one?
His countenance glowed, his thighs burned
and she melted to the ardor of his blazing eyes.
Hera traced his secret path to thunderclouds
over Boeotia and floated down herself
when Semele was barely pregnant, disguised
as sympathetic crone to a young girl swollen
by love from whom no lover could be found.
Hera fed Semele mistrust about her deceitful
spouse and Semele's swain, suggesting lover's deity
was but a ruse to wraps his arms around her,
despite Semele's defense how powerful his passion.
When Zeus came next, drawing her down to lie
with him, she pulled back, asking him to manifest
his godness. His glib reply but doubled doubt:
to show her would result in death since mortals
cannot withstand such glory, if any existed.
Finally relenting and regretting simultaneous,
Zeus let fall his outer human form and Semele
burst into flame as he had warned. Zeus reached in
and plucked his child from her flaming womb, sewing
it inside himself instead, doubly conceived Dionysus.
While in flight, last pregnant Zeus heard above
Semele's weakening cries was Hera's laughter.

45

Delphi

Apollo's temple landscape rises vertical
to emphasize his preference for sky,
framed by peaks, sun pierced clouds,
columned light, deeper vales,
dusky ravens crying overhead.

Breezes strum his woods like strings
stirring Muses from their dreams,
Castalia's only sacred citizens,
where water sculpts each stone
so slowly no one hears a sound.

Lovingly he plants young laurel trees
around his temenos, wanting only
holy aromatic leaves. If thus he slyly
has Daphne embracing him instead,
somehow this nymph so honored stays.

By the Rivers of Babylon

A thousand skeletons rattling in wind,
valley of dry bones said the prophet,
autumn in the courtyard of sadness
where fallen leaves rustle, wingless angels
after sunlight fled, all glory departed.

Those thousand skeletons were their dreams,
once green leaves mothered by wind
now brown before the desert's breath
says Ezekiel, whose visions of whirling wheels
are no longer chariots but bureaucracies

churning out armaments through smoke
of charnel houses fed by soldiers' arms
and legs blown off before they knew it,
before they even knew how to run.
You can hear their guardian angels weeping.

Prophets

for Dean Alan Jones

Some prophets are cantankerous, others gentle
but most end up sawn in half or thrown in wells.
With a scowl as he walked through Bethel,
Elisha made bears maul forty boys who mocked
his baldness. Nathan, not so confrontational,
softly wove Bathsheba's allegory where David,
having ravished Uriah's wife after her bath,
only recognized his inner wolf as anticlimax.

Whether seer or stargazer, if your portfolio
consists of talking donkeys and dreams of angels
climbing ladders heavenward, it takes
a thick-skinned herald to tell God's wrath
when his unfaithful prefer hearing flattery
to a dies irae. So imagine poets waxing lyrical
on acid rain and rivers running out of fish,
coral dying like bleached bones, an apocalypse

of climate shudders; where specters we fear most
are not uncontrollable wildernesses but our shadows
over earth, a desert where once was paradise.
Malthus may not have been a seer but more
an actuarial reckoner. He didn't count his chickens
before they hatched, especially if their shells
were dioxin weak. Blake saw his London darkened
by coal and laws of unintended consequences

where Satanic mills enslaved more than millstreams
and Marx saw visions of Jesus blessing poor folk
in gospels. No Song of Innocence but no hymn
of praise either. Baptizer John wore camel suede
and ate grasshopper sushi but he did not
have a riverside country club congregation,
preferring his head to be served on a platter
than to compromise with the Herods of this world.

Endymion

'Byron in Greece' Opera

Endymion, the shepherd boy,
loved by the moon, reflects her joy.
The moon won't touch his human flesh,
instead his mind she ravishes.

He cannot wait to fall asleep,
each day too long, each night too short.
One morning soon he won't awake,
his eyes still closed, his soul she'll take.

He dreamt last night she kissed his eyes
bathed in her light, inside he sighs.
There is no moon, the sky is bare
and yet in him she's everywhere.

The leaves will fall, the streams run dry,
the shepherd sleeps, he can't know why.
Forever hers hid in a cave,
he'll never age, Endymion.

Garden of Cyrus

for Hamid Moghadam

Cyrus made his garden at Pasargad
channeling water from purple Zagros,
planting his scented groves in ordered rows,
bringing water and light to his orchards
whose hundreds of trunks were sun gilded
and whose leaves rustled with languages
of many satrapies. Later kings fashioned
their great halls of a hundred columns
after this garden of Cyrus, whose empire
was rooted in earth but looked heavenward.
At night stars glimmered like fruit
hung high in his garden's branches,
and voices of fountains sang like choirs
of children under flowering trees. At sunset
and at dawn when shadowed air was cool
Cyrus, Great Gardener of Persia, stood alone
reflecting glorious sun, spreading his arms
to either far horizon. Even then
he hardly cast a shadow, instead
spreading light around the world.

Aristotle and Phyllis

Philosophers may love to think
they are immune to amatory impulses,
ultra rather than subrational, so when
Aristotle fell for Phyllis, lovely courtesan
of Athens half his age but twice as coy,
she made him pay with body and soul.
She taught not with cold theories of love
at thought's elevated altitudes but baser loci,
besotted as he was with love's fevered reality.
Aristotle, rich mind of his age, was humbled
to poor moping fool. If he really loved her,
Phyllis teased, he must crawl through Athens
on all fours with Phyllis riding on his back
for all to see devotion so plainly stated,
no lofty proposition few would find arrant
but lowest common denominator dominant.
He agreed and to the laughter of the mob
Phyllis rode triumphant on her philosopher,
young thighs straddling his old shoulders easily,
proving love is twice as wise as sophistry.

Danae

for John Felstiner

Gold comes from sunlight drop by drop
as Danae felt it warm her loins, a god
disguised can penetrate a keyhole.
Rembrandt surrounds her with a glow
enough to light her bed. Klimt renders
her ecstasy, hands kinked in pleasure,
eyes closed to what she feels, hair tangled,
cheeks rosy with coital flush, hot gold stream
entering between her open legs. If later
a golden child comes, Danae will cling
to its promise, treasuring hope to her chest.
Her breasts, nipples now erect to a god's lust,
will then flow with milk. Even in climax Danae
senses gold is not for keeping, humans only
pass it on, pretending to possess it for a few breaths.
Incorruptible when we are not, solid
when we are insubstantial, reflecting light
we absorb, we seek gold to contradict mortality.
Such golden miracles as this must have
priceless purposes, heroes engineered, Perseus
on his way to rescue kingdoms. Can Danae
growing old sustain this moment lifelong
as we remember her filled with a god?

Night Perfumes

for Pamela

When only moon and stars stroll
at night high above Granada,
hot summer dusks release perfumes
from a thousand hidden gardens.
Spanish jasmine, myrtle and gardenia
glow white, soft pearls set in emeralds,
eyes of night unveiled, their spices
excite lovers where soft breezes waft.

Around Alhambra's pools and arbors
fountains sound, and in their leafy nests
peacocks sleep to water songs, dreaming
of aquatic iris blue as turquoise eggs.
A nightingale hears her mate, ruiseñor,
in evening serenade, she flies to him
like a cloud wings through night sky
racing its own moon shadow.

A guitar plays somewhere, its notes
strings of roses whose petals fall
like warm tears on moonlit paths
when desire is a feast without tasting.
Surpassing flowers is my woman's smell
if she comes close enough to touch,
light wind lifting her scented hair into
my face and our seeking lips brush.

Auguries

for Emily Vermeule

Below Mycenae voices sing harvest
when wheat borrows gold from the sun,
not bird hymns but winged with harmony
needing no kithara to pluck grain threshed
by wind under fortresses crowning high hills.
Sunset waits for Atreus standing atop his palace,
his robe embroidered with lions, his great beard
gilded by last light. No enemy he can imagine
would dare assault his Zeus-bolted gates.
Stars soon to appear will measure his kingdom
from horizon to horizon, some like flowers
blooming in night fields of sky, other asterisms
crouching far below winter's white harbinger peaks
with fearful augury dark bull blood will not appease:
can we ever see our proud stones toppled to ruin
millennia hence where they will say of us
we must have been giants to build like this?

Chimaera

Three natures struggle for dominance within,
one heart shared by triple schismatic raging minds,
none succeeds in eliminating any common nature
because then it would but harm itself. Lion fears
snake at its distant tail weaving at its roaring,
snake fears goat most, sharp horns impaling,
goat fears lion lunging at its bearded throat,
each confounded head separated just enough
to not succeed in destroying natural enemies.
Only when one will directs can this monster move
forward without anarchy of its different members
if three sets of eyes focus on the same victim,
overlooking strange revulsions of its blood
flowing from hot lion to cold snake to tepid goat
as it circulates in grim battle through awkward
skin shuddering where hair and scales join.
Breathing fire like a smelter, its innards radiate
noxious flames from internal furnaces, scorching
its own iron entrails painlessly but setting fire
to all it touches. Only molten lead poured down
its throat could kill Chimaera, Bellerophon found
to his relief instructed by Athena, choking off
its breath, freeing Lycia and himself from curse.
Do monsters ever know what they are, solitary
disturbances of nature, strange harbingers of wrath
of gods at human hubris - hence their hybrid nature –
or are they merely angry at their mixed plight,
looking for like frustrated mating partners
as in myth Typhon and Echidne huddled together
to pass on their conjoined troubles to successors?
Monsters obey divine summons to punish us
for pride; we create them when we fail to stop
at boundaries set by gods. Thus our monsters meet
us, mirrored just beyond each outlaw threshold.

Dragonfly

for John Felstiner

Dragonfly landing in my garden
with a slow whir of cellophane wings,
afternoon sunlight broken into prisms,
dropping from bright skies you struggle,
profound aerobatics no longer easy.

I realize you come here to die.
A cool fountain welcomes, shadows
of roses still warmed by summer's end.
In your myriad eyes a thousand adventures reflect
skimming lakes in exuberant strength,

dances with zephyrs, landings on lily pads.
A naiad living under bubbles in green water
knows only fish songs, fins stirring silent currents,
deep visions none but tadpoles believe,
hearing rainfall pierce lake surfaces above,

soundwaves only an insect tympanum feels
but that was in spring almost a lifetime ago.
Unafraid of anything now, your head turns faintly
to me as I hover, your bold colors fading to gray
until neither of us has anything more to say.

Song of Solomon

for Pamela

It's how we remember first love
not closed in a room but outside.
Lavender fields freshly cut,
smelling sunlight on our skin,
cicada sounds slice purple air.

You undress in silhouette
graceful cedar with a lustful sun
behind you like a voyeur.
Loosing your hair on my shoulder
there is no turning back

when clumsy shyness flees
because instinct remembers
what the mind fumbles,
a million generations repeat
stag and doe leaping on hills.

We sleep till gentle dusk
leaving behind a soft hollow
in this field, grass not so much crushed
as pressed together sweetly
by our urgent tangle of limbs.

Psyche

for Carol Boggs

In antiquity to see a butterfly
meant a good soul off to Elysium,
only right to take our breath away
if it seems this being has none of its own.
Lepidoptera – insect class of butterflies -
have myriad wing scales, like umbrellas
held aloft, appearing lighter than air.
Hesperiidae, Pieridae, Heliconidae
are dispersed like old Greek demes,
every specie sharing hue and size,
wingspots, veins of different shapes,
their ease in winging over flowers
like airborne blooms themselves
defying all but imagination. Thus psyche
translates both soul and butterfly in Greek,
no flight weighed down by flesh and bone,
rarely still in sunlit moments hovering,
their journey long to far off better fields.

Cretan Memory

for Richard Martin

At Archanes bulls shuffle in shade
near vineyards, oddly remembering
moves from courtyard dances, leaping
gymnasts whose prayers in flight
were sometimes lighter than air
across taut backs arching away.

Cretan peaks may not all be horned
like Mount Jouktas, but their rocks
are just as hard as pavements
where bull dancers died, spinning
as they fell from sky, broken stars
gored and trampled as wine blood.

I saw old amphorae sleeping
in a deep well above Arvi
farmers only dug out yesterday,
having scraped away a villa
underneath millennia of soil
where so many dry years followed

Minoan plenty when white sails
brought gold from Egypt
with diorite cups, rock crystal gems
and sparkling emery from Naxos
for sculptors to rub away
anything that wasn't gentle.

Here, new Archanes wine
is sweet, fresh as springs running
down gorges, its amber color
drawn from afternoon sun
when workers splashed it
for me, flooding over glass.

I smelled that winery for at least
a mile, its exciting live ferment
transforming grape blood,
a familiar lust to what wolves
smelled on Mount Diktys
so long ago when antelope

fled lions raking their backs
and goats lifted bearded heads
hearing frantic hooves pass by.
Now you can only see them
frozen on carved stone rhytoi
from Kato Zakro or Palai Kastro.

Cretan landscapes are more silent
than when cries of a god born
echoed from caves so womb deep
their dark hunger was shelter enough
for baby Zeus. Now hikers
sweat along trails where myth lived,

mostly oblivious to sacred peaks
and consecrated groves so overgrown
with old wood where bees once hung
from singing hives around Mallia,
only a tumble of stones, its frescoes
disintegrated by earthquakes,

buried fragments known to spiders.
Crests of every high hill on Crete
disclose a blue Aegean horizon
where dolphins still roll in waves
even if you cannot see them,
dim and far away as Minos himself.

Ode to Pheidippides

for Sepp Gumbrecht

Pheidippides runs to Sparta
and back, three hundred miles
deerlike, hardly touching ground,
fleet light feet over several days
past purple shaded Corinth,

over Peloponnesian roads, too fast
for white hilled dust to settle
under Nemean oaks dropping acorns.
Sea winds cool his face, morning
springs keep him from thirst

through miles of changing landscapes
as his strong steps pull earth forward.
His herald's goal is seeking help
for outnumbered Greeks
whose looming enemy appears:

proud Xerxes bringing myriads
of strange-faced mercenary soldiers,
sweat smelling of spice and aloe
in a thousand ships from Asia.
Returning, sent next urgently

to Marathon, another weary hundred miles
over pine scented hills heated by sun,
he runs to where Persians anchor,
here a long blue bay curves away
on both sides to browed hills

sheltering vast Asian fleets at harbor
like a swell of fish caught in nets.
Unison feet of phalanxes crush
fennel fields, once clear streams
from Mount Penteli are muddied.

Down in Marathon valley
swords strike shields locked
in battle, hoplites groan against iron,
aliens cursing gods in incoherent names.
Blood flows into tidewater, salt to salt,

shades of death mounting everywhere,
victory of chaos over order,
as when griffins hunt stallions
or harpies seize carrion human flesh,
until heavier bronze Greek armor

withstands a rain of Persian blows
ringing against breastplates, invaders
pushed back inch by hardened inch.
Five days of flies gather on dead eyes,
faces distorted by anguish. At last

Greek voices outnumber Persian.
Where at first Persians were ants
gathering around a morsel of ripe fruit,
now they are overrun by Greek phalanxes.
Retreating to their ships, Persian voices

fade. One lone runner weaves
his way to Athens leagues away,
thirsty, staggering toward sunset.
Exhausted Pheidippides pants,
hot sun blistering his haggard face,

numb feet forgetting how to stop,
lungs ache with insufficient breath
as tunnel vision darkens sight.
His feet leaden, his heart is bursting
as he crosses Kephissos stream,

deaf to all but blood rushing in his ears.
Only his message carries him on
to Athens, that so many Persians,
uncountable like winter night stars,
were vanquished by so few Greeks,

that Marathon soil is fed by foreign blood
under crushed grass and broken shrubbery,
that Attica is safe again, aflame
no longer. But his legs now burn instead,
unable to carry him inside Athens' marble entry,

falling hard before Propylaion's white portal.
All faces, voices blur before him. Finally,
his glorious heart stops when his voice saves
its gasping words for last, his whisper
cries both victory and death in one breath.

Scents

Flaubert had intense epilectic moments,
synesthesia with starbursts of smell and light,
fireworks of taste and sound, lightning bolts
of touch that laid him flat with pain or pleasure
from exploding senses just before a seizure.
Rimbaud distilled poisons like absinthe
to be a poet seer, but sense memory
is often powerful enough on its own.
Take smell. A provocative scent
may stay hidden from conscious years,
others have no antecedent for memory.
Bending down to smell a star white lemon flower
where its espaliered branch seeks a terrace,
I remember childhood greenhouses
my grandmother loved to tend, because
growing outside was a small lemon tree
whose blooms were startling to a child.
Today's scent of lemon floret released older
ancestors of memory to parade before me.
Fresh cut grass reminds me of rolling
dizzily downhill on a new mown lawn
decades ago as oblique sun illuminated
golden poplars above emerald fields
my uncle had just cut. Now a whiff
of vanilla or spicy sandalwood recalls
milled soaps purchased in Arles markets
under a canopy of bright Provencal
summer sky dappled by high clouds.

Even a smell of sidewalks after rain
can last decades if I then see my earliest one
when I could barely walk, where glints
of sun made steam rise from pavements.
But more than all of these is her perfume
familiar even after years, lush gardenia
as on our wedding night, when her arms
enfold my neck and her breasts blossom
eternally like lotus against my eager skin.

Cannae

Hannibal's shadow may be invisible here
although Roman ground still shudders
at his name. From Cannae's citadel vista
low hills march horizonward to azure
Adriatic flatness. No thunder now
of Numidian cavalry sweeping right
or Aufidius river burbling down
at left, here only a trickle of itself.
Cicadas still complain of August heat
and dust blown hard from Africa.
Walking across this fearsome battlefield,
screams of hamstrung horses and men
lying round may no longer echo loud,
whitened crow-stripped bones no longer jut
from mangled earth, but awful memories
linger from at least fifty thousand
Roman corpses merciless Hannibal left behind,
a generation of Italy's manhood silenced.
Rocky soil is mostly hidden from view
because vineyards blanket all of Cannae.
Trellises sag across this battlefield
from heavy clusters hanging full, so one
wonders if after several millennia such red grapes
are still nourished by rusty Roman blood.

Adam and Eve by Masaccio

If Adam's feet are swollen trudging from Eden,
goaded by a flaming sword a saffron angel waves,
whose wouldn't be sore on such hard scrabble,
his toes had known but moss and ferns before.

He's bent now like a wasted arrow, ruddy from sweat,
hands covering face and eyes he does not want to see,
looking down because he cannot look up shamelessly.
He cannot even lead the way with Eve in front.

Gates of Paradise close after them, no glimpse
of green through stone portal, but words of judgment bell
through its arch, following them from behind. Its threshold
is higher as Adam steps down to baked and barren clay.

Eve anguishes at herself, weeping and laboring in pain
at divine pronouncements. She looks not at heaven
but her future, unbearable although she must bear
no unperishable body but only a half copy of herself.

Modesty covers her, her hands on breasts and loins
because this is where her life must go, motherhood
was not her choice or what she wanted in her name,
spitting out those apple seeds too late when sin germinated

inside her soul. While Eve covers her private parts
in futility, Masaccio hung huge genitals on naked Adam
for everyone in church to see. Perhaps like us his offspring,
exposed Adam has no recourse to any immortality but this.

Jacob's Ladder

for Bob Gregg

Stone pillow should be oxymoron
for dreaming, hard enough to make
rest impossible, stiffnecked for anyone
but stubborn Jacob, adamant character
who strove incessantly with everyone

on everything, whether genetic breeding
of herds to make a stronger strain -
Gregor Mendel learned it all from him -
or with Laban over marriage contracts
and even wrestling angels. But that night

he didn't seek advantage, only
a good night's sleep, forgetfulness
for once to unclench fists and rest
his wary eyes. Whether his eyes were open
or not, he saw impossible high ladders

stretching heavenward and bright beings
ascending, descending thereon. He knew
it was proleptic, since a loudspeaker
announced his future, more children
than he could count, commercial success

beyond measure his eternal epitaph.
Had Jacob only known that night
he saw escalators of Bergdorf Goodman
and Nieman Marcus in his future, sales staff
carrying ledgers in fluorescent light

for another summer evening sale
hearing cheerful harp glissande arpeggios.
Jacob built a limestone altar around
his pillow and named it Bethel,
House of God. Although he never
worshipped Mammon, only Yahweh

as long as he was Chosen, which was
writ forever, he held Almighty God
to that nocturnal contract. Dreaming Jacob
was a story singer whose gifts were legion,
wilier than Esau and ruddy Edom,

but he also dealt with others' envy for millennia,
a captive thrown in fiery furnaces, disallowed
to live in city limits, blamed for plagues
or driven out, stranger in a strange land,
herded into ovens wearing yellow stars.

Virtuoso prisoner, how could his fiddle sing
of far away Jerusalem, although his cantor kinder
danced from Beersheba to vaudeville, through Babylon
to Broadway, speakeasies where they could always beat
a raid, playing klezmer with an ironic note.

Jacob's ladder moves from place to place,
angels ready, heaven hovers near,
desert stones more carefully chosen
when dreams are harder to come by
than a diamond bargain from De Beers.

Jacob, looking up saw Orion constellation
known to him by older names like Gilgamesh,
mighty hunter Nimrud, no belt-hung sword
but a mighty phallus. Promised offspring, Jacob
anchored his ladder from heaven to earth and back.

La Dame à la Licorne

for W.S. Merwin

So many flowers this ground embroiders
from silk looms, millefiore swards of make believe
where rampant honeyed lions hold pennants,
golden hares converse with silver pheasants

under ferny garden trees flush in fruit
while smelling violets, rue or lilies,
weavers orchestrate each sensory gift
in panoramic detail. But equally in close up

one can count petals on marguerites
and find a hidden allegory in silence
or all those humble chamomiles crushed
like fragrant saviors pleading underfoot,

palanquins at forest edge whose lovers
absent themselves from view, canopies
drawn for privacy or merely inviting
speculation a highborn lady could brush off

as easily as that hand on her bodice
when she is coy, however smiling.
Rich tapestries narrate longing artfully,
wishful songs of troubadour to damsels,

hinting they are sought by unicorns,
old courtly loving somehow still in vogue
as long as brilliant tournaments honor
heraldry and troth. What splendid unicorns

whose lithe muscled rumps are parabolic,
glowing white, pure as snow until a ruby eye glints
of masked desire, and horns are gently lowered
to unleash wily heads in warmest ladies' laps.

Thus a unicorn horn is no weapon
in proximity to a virgin, wondering
which of them is more excited to be
touching, her eyes widen, his eyes close.

Turtledoves nest in roses, sylphs
scold foxes hunched in shrubs,
pards lick their own fur rosettes
like feline gardeners self pruning,

and if one finds a hissing serpent here
in this locked up hanging garden,
latent venom waiting for delivery,
innocence shuddering to fathom sin

when a unicorn can be caught only
by a virgin, it would be wholly out of place.
A bridal gift as this would euphemize
grave dangers beyond high garden walls.

Although if you look close enough
to see one papillon hover on a flower
in that tapestry corner, his tongue
kissing nectar, this might be enough

to remind that our ecstatic love
is also ever greedy, never sated,
and as much it yearns to be divine,
it roots in spicy decomposing earth.

Salome

She was set up to dance, not at all a vixen
like her depraved mother who pandered
Salome to a den of lechers that evening.
Even those hypocrites in priestly robes
who were already compromised, bought
by kingly bribes, could not look away.
Worst of all was drooling Herod,
who calculated how he could have her
at any cost, lust dancing before his eyes
since she was not really his daughter
and maybe not even his virginal niece
given his purloined wife's rumored habits.
Not technically incest if his rotten blood
did not already taint her, so whatever
fevered moves her mother made her rehearse
in private must have made old eyes pop
and a few other things beside if her glances
suggested she was fertile as a filly in first heat
begging for satisfaction. Of course, Salome
was only fifteen, hardly a ripe pomegranate
and knew nothing about love, only what
her mother prophesied how Herod that fool
would fall over himself to promise anything,
half his kingdom, although she only wanted
John's head on a platter, here and now.
Salome made no one happy in that dance
since every oath plummeted hellward
except John's, rising pure to heaven
carried by whitest wings, carrying with it
Salome's tears, her last happiness stolen.

Sirens

Wailing some otherwise unheard tragedy,
they pass us howling and we shiver,
hoping no one we know is headed
their way. Red lanterns flashing astern,

our pentekonter ship shuddering
in heavy wind, high shrill voice notes sound
in coloratura mode, breaking glass
that echoes through Messina's straits.

Steer the wheel some other way,
try not to listen to their anguish,
do not follow when they call,
singers only of destruction.

They may be inefficient at keeping life,
surrounded by death and harbingers
thereof, inured to suffering, having
seen plenty as they hover round,

en route to our emergency when we
are crushed between rocks and hard places,
sirens coming fast however unbidden by us.
Feathers unpreened, unrecognizable

faces even when bending close,
Odysseus doesn't see them anyway,
hogtied in stiffening ecstasy.
We put cold hands hard to these ears

we clog with beeswax, as Odysseus
commands, but look at him - drooling fool
who thinks it cannot unhinge his mind.
No way to monitor jarring pain

or regulate a pulse, no orderly here
where chaos rules, accidents abound
whose gurneys gather fast like flies. Even if
we could fall into siren eyes or be close

enough to feel hot breath, this is not just
any beauty bursting out but haunting song,
unendurable unless like immobile Odysseus
we could all journey to madness and return.

Sounion

A holy place where we rejoice coming from afar,
returning ships bow to Poseidon's shining
marble shrine, white like our sails against deep blue,
temple columns rising high from towered cliffs,

here Menelaus built an altar to heroic Phrontis.
After a climb uphill, where miles away one could see
Athena's gleaming speartip and her helmet's crest,
we pay homage to Attica's dual guardians with libations

of oil and water overboard or poured down precipices
where waiting waves respond below. Even if
much later Byron writes Childe Harold, champion
of Hellenic memory, inscribing his name as well

in Sounion stone so many others imitate, unwise
precedent and less desired canto, his pilgrim age
was honored. We revisit without stylus to record
although wayfaring Pausanias left his own account.

Cormorants wing between our masted fleet,
birds Poseidon hears within his temple columns
while resting in his portico. Down here waves
whisper his name my ship's black hull can only praise.

What shells are left against his shore, where triton echoes,
nautilus sings and conches roar, Poseidon over geologic
time dissolves them into lime, later brings them back
transformed as temple marble sentinels for Sounion.

Kithairon

Pruning wild limbs on Mt. Kithairon
is no impediment to a vine god,
dismemberment to him is temporary
like the faith of mortals.
Here on this ivy mountain
some see his beard in the clouds
or his thigh knotted in a root.

But in the eyes of Pentheus
pruning was in troubled wood,
powerless to take root again
since his sad mother has both
knit and unknit the cloth of him.
Is it wind we hear howling on Kithairon?

Gyges

Gyges is young for a spearman,
guardian of royal treasure, here
Queen of Sardis, prize of Lydia,
jewel of Asia in his king's crown.
Witless, shameless King Candaule
brags his wife surpasses all in beauty,
doesn't Gyges agree? But then
his king argues, how can his soldier,
since Gyges hasn't seen her naked?

King Candaule forces Gyges to hide
inside her tent against all decency,
making him involuntary voyeur
commanding both mind and manhood,
threatening death unless his guard
sees her beauty for himself. At first
Gyges cannot look, but emerging
slowly from her bath, no queen turns
so provocatively by torchlight,

revealing all her loveliness:
long thighs stretched before
his reluctant but unprotesting eyes,
thick tousled hair lit up from behind,
firelight dancing on her flesh
as if to ravish her in flame,
eyes flashing with unknown desires,
bare arms white as Sardian marble,
lithe as a mountain hunting lioness,

breasts bending down like fruit
whose rosy nipples point for a kiss
as she inches ever closer, and
he silently agrees, no woman
could be more lovely. Even
young Gyges is aflame, trembling,
until his lovely queen strides close
and suddenly tears away his curtained
hiding place. Gyges gasps in fear

as this haughty queen of Sardis
feigns to call another guard.
Burning with anger, she knew
her husband's lack of shame.
She challenges Gyges with a choice:
either he quickly kills King Candaule
for his disrespect of her, must
spear him like a marauding beast,
or be killed himself. "What is more,

Gyges," she whipsers, so lovely naked,
"You can be my king instead" reasoning
as she wraps warm arms around him
and gazing in his eyes to convince him.
"Put that spear to better use,"
she places his hand on her womb.
Gyges makes a sensible choice,
skewering Candaule when he comes
in self-congratulating hubris,

then taking his place to reign as king,
much wiser than foolish Candaules.
Gyges wisely reined for many years,
protector of both her dignity and country,
finding her his loyal fervent queen,
not only wiser than her prior husband
but far more, as prized for her mind
as beauty, with her strong legs saddling
him for decades in that warm bed.

Ikarios

Dionysus lands his vinous ship himself in Greece,
tiller steered in only one hand because a kantharos
occupies his other. Slurred voice blaming pirates
or pilots, difficult to pronounce such difference,
he uproots his mast laden with heavy grapes,
carrying it inland to a welcome village
where he is house guest to Ikarios. Planting
his vine in Ikarian fields, instructing his host
in matters viticultural - except how much
a mortal can tipple - Dionysus sleeps it off,
one arm like a vine around young Akme,
hostess daughter who found guest irresistible.
Meanwhile new vigneron Ikarios
shares new vintages with fellow villagers
who trip away befuddled, staggering in fear
only knowing they have lost control. Ikarios
is slain with barrel staves, losing all but smile:
home, life and daughter, while god and girl dance
off to woods, which only proves such ample gifts
from gods to men must be carefully considered.
What elevates a god, however generous,
might not be apotheosis for a mortal.

Oedipus and the Sphinx

for George Brown

Oedipus cannot unshackle destiny
whose storm limps towards Thebes
where wings like a beating Fury wait.
Which monster blocks roads,
homicidal sphinx or parricidal prince?

Sphinx and prince should see themselves
mirrored in each other, enigmas of hubris
challenging authority, auspices
of doom, bringers of chaos to a polis.
A hero who can confound a sphinx

but cannot solve his own riddle,
Oedipus blindly plants in Jocasta's womb,
same that bore him, son and mother hobbled
by impious wills, unable to ask questions or seek
answers, compounding half belief in oracles.

All his conscious life obsessed with flight
as in a nightmare where one cannot outrun
slow death, Oedipus barely remembers
his infancy when he crawled on Kithairon
on all fours like a beast chained to fate.

If a Sphinx flees howling from such crossroads
it is not because she bows to a greater intellect –
asking crippled Oedipus who needs three feet
was a birdbrained impediment – but rather
because she feared facing greater monsters.

Circe

Again, men become beasts outside
until Circe frightens Odysseus
when godlike wayfarers make magic
in uprooted moly, much like mandrakes.
Uninvited transformations
are journeys, our years for heroes
bedding goddesses. Helping gods
want perplexity in heroes.

Heroes in perplexity want gods helping.
Goddesses bedding heroes
for years, our journeys are
transformations uninvited.
Mandrakes, like much moly uprooted
in magic, make wayfarers godlike
when Odysseus frightens Circe
until outside beasts become men again.

Oresteia

Watchman, tell us from constellations
stretching from dark horizon to horizon,
war chariots drawn by starry horses,
night dreams of women nursing snakes,
or blazing boats whose nebular sails
are blown by unseen gods in Magellanic
clouds, whether to guard high heaven
or one's own heart and home is easier.
Agamemnon and his kin can come
to grief, as much from their own doing
as by destiny none desired, in fact
from which all fled, thus fulfilling.
If our wisdom must come by suffering
ton pathei mathos, as choruses sing,
what does it teach beyond patience,
humility, justice in our hopes?
Furies cannot touch us when we kill
passions in ourselves, such hubris
as this our soul's bloodhounds find,
even if dying for love, or we thought
was love, delusion in masquerade
when we strike others only to wound
ourselves as much or more instead.
Ask Orestes what furious voices said
when he from Argos to Athens fled:
Was it wishing clemency for self
or revenge for others when Orestes
wondered if his pursuing Furies bred
on blood and was he their father?

Lucretius on Nature

for Mary Beard

If Lucretius pondering on nature muses
what makes eagles seek dizzier heights
to hang on, or moles churn deep soil to treasure,
bees chase flower perfumes for their alchemy,
or flies sleuth something dying to cling on,
concluding they are much alike, common
instincts providing each their different glory,
how might he wed what seems paradox
in nature but, peering closer, reconciles?
So wisdom needs a fool to be transformed,
love needs urgency of desire to burn all
who fall fatally into orbits of Mars and Venus.
Foliage requires a modicum of sun to live
and then diminished light to burn, writhe
through many colors, yellow and carmine,
triumphs of growing darkness over daylight
before trees can let them go to start again.
If Charon poles his skiff through dark waters
in search of souls that Hades always needs
for citizens, knowing he'll never finish
as long as mortal lovers love and die,
cycles that cannot arrest their movements,
every level either visible or measureless,
stags dancing gracefully around their does,
uncuttable atoms pirouette around each other
just like galaxies reel in brighter courtship.
But when stars die, exploding in flame, what gods
gather to warm their hands around the embers?

Golden Ass

after Juvenal

Let Isis offer breakfasts of roses to halt our braying,
so ask her to transform not only language but lifestyle,
we're bruised enough from religion's kicks. Whether
sorcery bends bodies more than minds is arguable,
but hardly laughable to donkeys or us despite
ironies of how we are more like them than gods.
Especially true when love potions or legal outcomes
  depend on jiggering their objects for desired results.
Lead curse tablets and philtres share a fierce common
spark: irrational incentives to pay dearly for desire.
Which ingredient is really efficacious? In love potions
it has to be most difficult to find, such as pubic hairs
from live wolves in Dacia during full moon
(may Fortuna be with you to obtain these trifles).
Pharmakia dilates your eyes - no bovine Juno -
but worse, dilutes resolve, as Ulysses found.
  Hardly worth epoptes when you have to sleep it off.
Long before sacrifice became a test of sanctity,
gods grumbling with thunder, victims slithering
off altars when no one seemed to care or were
paid to look elsewhere, religion became cynical.
Roman priests always prayed with one eye open.

Wedding Song

Epithalamion for Hilary and Brad

Sappho sang at weddings in all seasons,
but sometimes her favorite calendar
for bride and groom was at the cusp of winter
when leaves spindle precious light to gold outside
while love's fire burns hot inside the soul's hearth.
Sappho craved olive harvest when the ripe black fruit
leaps eagerly from high cold branches into baskets
to be baked in warm bread. West winds bluster
with cold strength bursting through winter's portals,
evening stars glitter overhead and an ivory moon
races between silver clouds. Embraces keep you warm
when robust weather spins the world on its axis.
We remember you as children excited to shout over
November wind surging against you like an animal.
Days are short, surely a good thing to wish in winter,
for we dream better when the night is long,
yes, blessing lovers when the night is long.

Alberti Numbers

Nihil est enim simul et inventum et perfectum.

for Anthony Grafton

Plato's forms were shapeshifters for Alberti,
geometric constellations of ideas in polygons
spinning across night skies in his domed head,

noiseless because their machinations encountered
little friction from vectors of air while multiplying
sides. Tetrahedra became octohedra, dodecahedra
in his dreams, thus less angular, more Aristotelian,
not precisely following eidos but morph, metatheses

of forma if lions could change to leopards, whatever
nature allowed in some iconic agency, a rounder
bestiary beyond mere istoria of variety in which fowl,
small dogs, birds, horses, sheep now intersected circles.
Centaurs were more anomalies than alchemies.
Everything had its dignity, harmonizing together
even antitheses like his façade at Santa Maria Novella
where all lines converged invisibly at horizons

at least inside his ordered head, stonemasons almost
forgiven when they could not duplicate proportions.
His new volute scrolls softened sharp-edged basilicas,
hinting Archimedes on spiral infinity expanding
above parallel arcades. Painters did not always like
his mirrors where, like Narcissus, weakness reflected
but they proved he knew mythology and Pythagoras,
like Vitruvius his kindred soul, although Alberti's
numbers had to wait for nature to give them flesh.
Alberti understood why Zeuxis painted grapes so true
that birds pecked, painting his composite Helen
because no single model satisfied his higher goal:
Beauty herself more real than her earthly shadows.

Library of Babylon

for Mike Keller

King Nabonidus started his collecting early
as a boy, clay tablets from crumbling cities,
exotic parchments made from lionskins -
cuneiform looking like what lion claws raked -
or sifting traces of meteoric dust writ
by fallen stars with mysterious whispers
recorded across deep Euphrates nights.

He was not at all like his hyperactive father
who was bored by his droning seers,
Nebuchadnezzar who gathered gold
treasures, temple candlesticks, slave girls
who could dance on their fingertips,
playing tambours with their toes
while he crushed empires like game pieces.

Nabonidus preferred his bookishness,
retiring to his endless palace archives,
it was Gilgamesh his scribes copied best.
But then his son Belshazzar had no time
to augment the Library of Babylon,
his only contribution was ephemeral
handwriting on a wall before vanishing.

Garden of Alkinous

for Ted Kooser

Alkinous plants his orchard in a place
either nonexistent or only Homer knew,
but a garden some remember as a park,
including mine, its child by inspiration.

Hedged in by buddleia for butterflies,
a library of nectar for their tastes,
papilion purple for swallowtails, white
flower clusters for Vanessa atalanta,

although I never see Parnassius apollonius
who love mountains, or those Troides
poison-eating ones since aristolochia vines
cling elsewhere. Tongues probing iris trumpets,

butterflies are welcome, bits of floating sky.
Acre enough for winds from all directions,
each breeze loving different trees, pitiless
north wind boundaries fir and taxus yew,

warm south wind lulls eugenia and waving pine,
balmy west stirs jasmine, quince and citrus,
east feeds arbutus, liquid amber, hydrangea,
trees by each wind craved, fondled, kissed.

West wind comes from sun-warmed oceans,
oblique light through rain or mist, moss wearing
diamond water droplets, shining stone drinks
rain brought by zephyrs to singing fountains.

Wisteria tumbles praising ferny trellises,
birds announce in morning light what bees love:
borage, thyme, achillea to nurse bare feet,
bold lemon blooms adjacent to its fruit.

Heliotrope, alyssum fall like waterfalls
from courtyard pots, poppies rise above them,
gladeoli unsheathe flowered swords to pierce
only air, ivy entwines artemisia and daphne.

Campanula binds up pelargonium,
ascending foxglove and hollyhock stalks,
replacing their downward hued bells
with its own upturned white face.

Hellebore sobers goats, slowing
their frantic dancing to a sedate pace
so they can avoid oleander spears
entangling twisted horns and beards.

Primroses disperse sweetest odors,
attracting dryads to collect them
at new moon, keeping melancholy at bay
and dryads in trees to make them healthy.

Laurel grows true at my garden center
endowing berried wreaths for Muses,
underneath its upward bowing branches
white sorrel spreads endearing flowers.

Spring showers make rainbow promises to buds,
seedlings present new leaves in miniature,
iridescent green like hummingbird breasts,
translucent as tulip petals or almond flowers.

Summer welcomes robust bees in symphony
hustling pollen from clover carpets underfoot,
July warmth desires to nuzzle velvet peaches
or nurture zinnias bursting with a zillion suns.

Fall fattens cherry fruit while loosening stems
until gravity wins, persimmons blushing
at their weight, sympathetic leaves watch
sunlight hide in alchemies of gold and red.

Winter prunes my deadwood with its storms,
soil contracts with cold, clouds cover
goosebump skies with coats, hibernating
night brings sleep to bulbs and deeper roots.

Pear leaves curl by following inner spirals
bent by internal numbers, phylotaxis following
light, but their pendant fruit swell with sugars
under skin as if pregnant, doubly parabolic.

Pomegranate blares red flowers multiplied,
every one, brighter inside, bears luscious seed
filled with ruby blood, Persephone's undoing,
their dark acerbic stains dye her maiden's dress.

Apples changing color from spring to fall
after flowers burst, toss their petals like coins,
green at birth but gradually sharing red, storing
sweetness in their round red domes, hardly misers.

Figs hide under heavy leaves, their modest nature
since they also conceal flowers inside, but this
is for protection until they ripen, when birds
purloin them for their fruitful health.

Olives rest along their dancing branches,
leafy silvered heralds of peaceful harvest
until sunlight turns their tannins black
and breezes shake them down to ground.

Grapes proliferate in clusters among vines
that climb wherever possible, each purpling fruit
jostling neighbors, light passing through,
gregarious since joy loves wine's company.

Rose unfolds many layers, perfumed texts
for us to read love letters in Aphrodite's
words, lavender, delphinium and salvia rising
underneath her lilied feet, dittany in her hands

to assure wounds made in this world are healed
from a garden loved alike by gods and humans.
So Epikouros sent his students to understand
that victors' wreaths from trees were only fleeting.

Gold chrysanthemum, late autumn solace, gives way
to cyclamen, crocus bows to violet and anemone,
blue hyacinth to geranium, parades of seasons
always changing, never tiring, ever humbling

as a gardener knows each year gains momentum
on its own, also tending us whose duties
are to suborn tares and water as needed, whose
long reward in loving beauty is to learn.